2016 SQA Past Papers & Hodder Gibson Model Papers With Answers

National 5
BUSINESS MANAGEMENT

Model Paper, 2014, 2015 & 2016 Exams

HODDER
GIBSON
AN HACHETTE UK COMPANY

This book contains the official SQA 2014, 2015 and 2016 Exams for National 5 Business Management, with associated SQA-approved answers modified from the official marking instructions that accompany the paper.

In addition the book contains a model paper, together with answers, plus study skills advice. This paper, which may include a limited number of previously published SQA questions, has been specially commissioned by Hodder Gibson, and has been written by experienced senior teachers and examiners in line with the new National 5 syllabus and assessment outlines. This is not SQA material but has been devised to provide further practice for National 5 examinations.

Hodder Gibson is grateful to the copyright holders, as credited on the final page of the book, for permission to use their material. Every effort has been made to trace the copyright holders and to obtain their permission for the use of copyright material. Hodder Gibson will be happy to receive information allowing us to rectify any error or omission in future editions.

Hachette UK's policy is to use papers that are natural, renewable and recyclable products and made from wood grown in sustainable forests. The logging and manufacturing processes are expected to conform to the environmental regulations of the country of origin.

Orders: please contact Bookpoint Ltd, 130 Park Drive, Milton Park, Abingdon, Oxon OX14 4SE. Telephone: (44) 01235 827720. Fax: (44) 01235 400454. Lines are open 9.00–5.00, Monday to Saturday, with a 24-hour message answering service. Visit our website at www.hoddereducation.co.uk. Hodder Gibson can be contacted direct on: Tel: 0141 333 4650; Fax: 0141 404 8188; email: hoddergibson@hodder.co.uk

This collection first published in 2016 by
Hodder Gibson, an imprint of Hodder Education,
An Hachette UK Company
211 St Vincent Street
Glasgow G2 5QY

Typeset by Aptara, Inc.

Printed in the UK

A catalogue record for this title is available from the British Library

ISBN: 978-1-4718-9103-8

3 2 1

2017 2016

Introduction

Study Skills – what you need to know to pass exams!

Pause for thought

Many students might skip quickly through a page like this. After all, we all know how to revise. Do you really though?

Think about this:

"IF YOU ALWAYS DO WHAT YOU ALWAYS DO, YOU WILL ALWAYS GET WHAT YOU HAVE ALWAYS GOT."

Do you like the grades you get? Do you want to do better? If you get full marks in your assessment, then that's great! Change nothing! This section is just to help you get that little bit better than you already are.

There are two main parts to the advice on offer here. The first part highlights fairly obvious things but which are also very important. The second part makes suggestions about revision that you might not have thought about but which WILL help you.

Part 1

DOH! It's so obvious but …

Start revising in good time

Don't leave it until the last minute – this will make you panic.

Make a revision timetable that sets out work time AND play time.

Sleep and eat!

Obvious really, and very helpful. Avoid arguments or stressful things too – even games that wind you up. You need to be fit, awake and focused!

Know your place!

Make sure you know exactly **WHEN and WHERE** your exams are.

Know your enemy!

Make sure you know what to expect in the exam.

How is the paper structured?

How much time is there for each question?

What types of question are involved?

Which topics seem to come up time and time again?

Which topics are your strongest and which are your weakest?

Are all topics compulsory or are there choices?

Learn by DOING!

There is no substitute for past papers and practice papers – they are simply essential! Tackling this collection of papers and answers is exactly the right thing to be doing as your exams approach.

Part 2

People learn in different ways. Some like low light, some bright. Some like early morning, some like evening / night. Some prefer warm, some prefer cold. But everyone uses their BRAIN and the brain works when it is active. Passive learning – sitting gazing at notes – is the most INEFFICIENT way to learn anything. Below you will find tips and ideas for making your revision more effective and maybe even more enjoyable. What follows gets your brain active, and active learning works!

Activity 1 – Stop and review

Step 1

When you have done no more than 5 minutes of revision reading STOP!

Step 2

Write a heading in your own words which sums up the topic you have been revising.

Step 3

Write a summary of what you have revised in no more than two sentences. Don't fool yourself by saying, "I know it, but I cannot put it into words". That just means you don't know it well enough. If you cannot write your summary, revise that section again, knowing that you must write a summary at the end of it. Many of you will have notebooks full of blue/black ink writing. Many of the pages will not be especially attractive or memorable so try to liven them up a bit with colour as you are reviewing and rewriting. **This is a great memory aid, and memory is the most important thing.**

Activity 2 – Use technology!

Why should everything be written down? Have you thought about "mental" maps, diagrams, cartoons and colour to help you learn? And rather than write down notes, why not record your revision material?

What about having a text message revision session with friends? Keep in touch with them to find out how and what they are revising and share ideas and questions.

Why not make a video diary where you tell the camera what you are doing, what you think you have learned and what you still have to do? No one has to see or hear it, but the process of having to organise your thoughts in a formal way to explain something is a very important learning practice.

Be sure to make use of electronic files. You could begin to summarise your class notes. Your typing might be slow, but it will get faster and the typed notes will be easier to read than the scribbles in your class notes. Try to add different fonts and colours to make your work stand out. You can easily Google relevant pictures, cartoons and diagrams which you can copy and paste to make your work more attractive and **MEMORABLE**.

Activity 3 – This is it. Do this and you will know lots!

Step 1

In this task you must be very honest with yourself! Find the SQA syllabus for your subject (www.sqa.org.uk). Look at how it is broken down into main topics called MANDATORY knowledge. That means stuff you MUST know.

Step 2

BEFORE you do ANY revision on this topic, write a list of everything that you already know about the subject. It might be quite a long list but you only need to write it once. It shows you all the information that is already in your long-term memory so you know what parts you do not need to revise!

Step 3

Pick a chapter or section from your book or revision notes. Choose a fairly large section or a whole chapter to get the most out of this activity.

With a buddy, use Skype, Facetime, Twitter or any other communication you have, to play the game "If this is the answer, what is the question?". For example, if you are revising Geography and the answer you provide is "meander", your buddy would have to make up a question like "What is the word that describes a feature of a river where it flows slowly and bends often from side to side?".

Make up 10 "answers" based on the content of the chapter or section you are using. Give this to your buddy to solve while you solve theirs.

Step 4

Construct a wordsearch of at least 10 × 10 squares. You can make it as big as you like but keep it realistic. Work together with a group of friends. Many apps allow you to make wordsearch puzzles online. The words and phrases can go in any direction and phrases can be split. Your puzzle must only contain facts linked to the topic you are revising. Your task is to find 10 bits of information to hide in your puzzle, but you must not repeat information that you used in Step 3. DO NOT show where the words are. Fill up empty squares with random letters. Remember to keep a note of where your answers are hidden but do not show your friends. When you have a complete puzzle, exchange it with a friend to solve each other's puzzle.

Step 5

Now make up 10 questions (not "answers" this time) based on the same chapter used in the previous two tasks. Again, you must find NEW information that you have not yet used. Now it's getting hard to find that new information! Again, give your questions to a friend to answer.

Step 6

As you have been doing the puzzles, your brain has been actively searching for new information. Now write a NEW LIST that contains only the new information you have discovered when doing the puzzles. Your new list is the one to look at repeatedly for short bursts over the next few days. Try to remember more and more of it without looking at it. After a few days, you should be able to add words from your second list to your first list as you increase the information in your long-term memory.

FINALLY! Be inspired...

Make a list of different revision ideas and beside each one write **THINGS I HAVE** tried, **THINGS I WILL** try and **THINGS I MIGHT** try. Don't be scared of trying something new.

And remember – "FAIL TO PREPARE AND PREPARE TO FAIL!"

National 5 Business Management

The course

The National 5 Business Management course should enable you to develop:

- knowledge and understanding of the ways in which society relies on business to satisfy our needs
- an insight into the systems that organisations use to ensure customers' needs are met
- enterprising skills and attributes by providing you with opportunities to explore realistic business situations
- financial awareness through business contexts
- an insight into how organisations organise their resources for maximum efficiency and to improve their overall performance
- an awareness of how external influences impact on organisations.

How the course is graded

The grade you finally get for National 5 Business Management depends on three things:

- the three internal Unit Assessments you do in school or college: "Understanding Business", "Management of People and Finance", and "Management of Marketing and Operations"; these don't count towards the final grade, but you must have passed them before you can get a course award and then a final grade
- your Assignment – this is submitted in April for marking by SQA and counts for 30% of your final grade
- the exam you sit in May – this counts for 70% of your final grade.

General advice

Although National 5 Business Management is a new qualification, it does draw most of its topics and content from the Standard Grade and Intermediate 2 Business Management courses. When studying the National 5 Business Management course and preparing for the external assessment, you should take account of previous advice issued by SQA in the External Assessment Reports prepared by the Principal Assessors for Standard Grade and Intermediate 2 qualifications.

Command words

It is often the case that candidates in the exam misunderstand what the question is asking them as they don't realise the importance of what is called the "Command Word". For example, if a question asks you to **identify** something, you only need to say what it is. However, if the question asks you to **describe** it, then you need to give some of the main features.

Example 1

Question: *Identify a source of finance for a business.*

1 mark

Acceptable answer: *A source of finance could be a Bank Loan.*

This answer will receive a mark as it does what the command word **identify** has asked.

Example 2

Question: *Describe a source of finance for a business.*

1 mark

Acceptable answer: *A loan from a bank which can be repaid with interest, over a period of time.*

In this case, where the command word is **describe**, there would be no marks awarded for the answer given in Example 1. You need to include some features of a bank loan (describe it) in order to get the mark. Remember, it is good practice to always answer in sentences.

So make sure you read the question carefully, checking the command word to see how you need to write your answer.

Context

Section 1 questions in the exam will provide you with a short piece of stimulus material, sometimes called a case study, with information about a small or medium sized business. The questions that follow will mostly relate to the case study and your answers should reflect the context given.

For example, if the case study is about a charity, then your answers should relate to a charity.

Example 3

Question: *Give an objective for the RSPCA.*   *1 mark*

Acceptable answer: *To promote animal welfare.*

Because the RSPCA is a charity there are a number of objectives that would not be suitable for them. For example, you would get no marks for saying an objective would be to make as much profit as possible.

Remember to relate all your answers to the business or organisation from the case study.

Marks

Check the number of marks for each question. Too often candidates write too much or too little. If there is only one mark available then you only need to make one point. It might be safer to give two just in case, but only if you have time. If there are four marks available, then you need to make four points to get full marks.

Check to make sure that you have made enough points in your answer to get full marks.

Topic areas

Understanding Business and Marketing are areas where candidates normally do well in exams. However, Finance proves tricky for a lot of students, and, to a lesser extent, so do Human Resources and Operations. There is no way to avoid questions on these topics, so you will need to learn what is contained in each.

Finance

There are only five parts to finance: sources of finance, break-even, cash budgeting, profit statement and technology.

For sources of finance you only need to be aware of where the organisation can get money from. Remember, this can be either to invest in the business or to overcome a cash flow problem, so make sure you understand which you should write about, as the acceptable answers may be different for different questions.

For break-even, you need to memorise the formula for calculating contribution and break-even. Once you have done this, these questions should be fairly straightforward. Don't be put off by the use of numbers. The calculations you may be asked to carry out are relatively simple and you will be able to use a calculator.

When looking at cash budgets in a question, it is always better to read left to right rather than up and down. Look for trends, such as a source of income going down, or a cost that is increasing. These would show potential problems which the business should worry about.

Human resources

Candidates often confuse what is included under each heading for recruitment and selection.

- **Recruitment**

  It is generally accepted that the recruitment stage involves job analysis, job description, person specification, the decision about whether to recruit internally or externally, and, finally, the advertisement of the job.

- **Selection**

  Here you will be expected to give answers about selection methods. These could include application forms/CVs, references, interviews and the various forms of testing available.

Remember that the recruitment stage is about the job and the selection stage is about picking the right person!

Operations

The main problem encountered by candidates is what is meant by quality. There are only two methods you need to know about.

- **Quality control**

  This is a simple system where the quality of raw materials is checked at the start of production, and the quality of the finished product is checked at the end.

- **Quality management**

  Here quality is checked at every stage from carrying out market research to learn what the customers need from the product, to providing quality after-sales service.

Problem answers

Some of the answers you might give to a question are not suitable for gaining marks. Try not to use answers such as "quicker", "easier", "more efficient", "saves time", "saves money" as these do not attract marks. They are *relative terms* and if you do use them you must show what you are comparing them to.

Example 4

Question: *Outline an advantage of using spreadsheets in Finance.* **1 mark**

Acceptable answer: *Formulas in the spreadsheet will carry out calculations automatically.*

You would not get a mark for saying it is faster than doing calculations by hand.

Always use business terminology in your answers – this is far more likely to get you the marks!

Good luck!

A lot of what you will learn in National 5 Business Management is common sense. As a consumer and a member of society you are already aware of most of the course content. The challenge is to make sure you understand the terms used. Hard work and good preparation go a long way, so keep calm and don't panic! GOOD LUCK!

NATIONAL 5

Model Paper

Whilst this Model Paper has been specially commissioned by Hodder Gibson for use as practice for the National 5 exams, the key reference documents remain the SQA Specimen Paper 2013 and the SQA Past Papers 2014, 2015 and 2016.

National Qualifications
MODEL PAPER

Business Management

Duration — 1 hour and 30 minutes

Total marks — 70

SECTION 1 — 30 marks

Attempt BOTH questions.

SECTION 2 — 40 marks

Attempt ALL questions.

Before attempting the questions you must check that your answer booklet is for the same subject and level as this question paper.

Read all questions carefully before attempting.

On the answer booklet, you must clearly identify the question number you are attempting.

Use **blue** or **black** ink.

You may use a calculator.

Before leaving the examination room you must give your answer booklet to the Invigilator. If you do not, you may lose all the marks for this paper.

HODDER
GIBSON
LEARN MORE

MARKS

SECTION 1 — 30 marks

Attempt BOTH questions

Roadwise Driver Training

Roadwise Driver Training, based in Aberdeen, is the largest independent driver training provider in the North East of Scotland.

Roadwise Driver Training was established in 1994 by founding manager Dave Watson, a former Police Class 1 Driver and Driving Instructor. Along with former business partner and police colleague, Roddie Munro, he developed Roadwise. It is now a leader in the field of driver training in the UK.

Roadwise is not only at the cutting edge of driver training but also broke new ground by becoming the first social enterprise driver training provider. Profit generated by Roadwise directly supports the work of Aberdeen Foyer who work to prevent and reduce youth homelessness and unemployment in Aberdeen and Aberdeenshire.

Safety is imbedded in every aspect of Roadwise from driving lessons or Under 17 tuition for learner drivers to skid training, defensive driving and road familiarisation as part of corporate packages tailor-made for companies.

Source – roadwisedrivertraining.co.uk

You should note that although the following questions are based on the case study above, you will need to make use of knowledge and understanding you have gained whilst studying the Course.

1. (a) (i) From the case study, identify the market segments Roadwise targets. **2**

   (ii) Outline the benefits of having different products for different customers. **3**

   (b) Describe the costs and benefits of off the job training for an organisation. **4**

   (c) Outline the benefits of Roadwise having a website for its business. **4**

   (d) (i) From the case study, identify the sector of industry that Roadwise operates in. **1**

   (ii) Describe the sector identified in (d) (i). **1**

   Total marks **15**

MARKS

Angus Soft Fruits Ltd is one of the leading suppliers of strawberries, raspberries, blueberries and blackberries to UK retailers. The business was established in 1994 with the objective of benefiting both customers and growers through direct contact between the two.

Angus Soft Fruits Ltd has a strict ethical policy which sets out minimum standards expected of grower-suppliers. The business takes its responsibility to the natural environment very seriously. It undertakes regular audits of its grower-suppliers to ensure that they are achieving and in the majority of cases exceeding industry standards.

It controls every aspect of the supply chain from propagation of plants to delivery to our customers' depots to ensure consumer quality expectations are exceeded. To achieve this it employs a team of specialists with detailed product knowledge.

You should note that although the following questions are based on the case study above, you will need to make use of knowledge and understanding you have gained whilst studying the Course.

2. (a) Outline the benefits to Angus Soft Fruits Ltd of having a strict ethical policy.   3

    (b) (i) From the case study identify methods Angus Soft Fruits uses to ensure quality.   2

         (ii) Describe the benefits for Angus Soft Fruits in providing quality products.   2

    (c) Angus Soft Fruits Ltd employ a team of specialists to help achieve its aims.

         Describe steps involved in the recruitment process.   3

    (d) (i) From the case study, identify the type of organisation that Angus Soft Fruits operates.   1

         (ii) Give 3 features of this type of business.   2

    (e) Identify sources of finance for Angus Soft Fruits.   2

                                                                 Total marks   15

MARKS

SECTION 2 – 40 marks
Attempt ALL questions

3. (a) Describe the benefits of using a bank loan for an organisation.   2

    (b) State 2 fixed costs for an organisation.   2

    (c) Using the following information, calculate the Net Profit of the business.   2
        Sales   £280,000
        Production costs   £120,000
        Other expenses   £85,000

    (d) Justify the use of cash budgets for an organisation.   4

                                                    Total marks   10

4. (a) Outline methods a business could use when selecting new employees.   2

    (b) Compare 2 types of payment systems used by organisations.   2

    (c) Identify 3 areas of discrimination that are not allowed under the Equality Act 2010.   3

    (d) Describe the employers' responsibilities under the Health and Safety at Work Act.   3

                                                    Total marks   10

5. (a) Outline the stages of the product life cycle.   4

    (b) Describe methods of field research, which could be used by an organisation.   4

    (c) Identify 2 considerations an organisation should make when launching a new product.   2

                                                    Total marks   10

6. (a) Explain why batch production would be the most suitable for an organisation such as Baxter's.   2

    (b) Compare quality control with quality management.   2

    (c) Outline the benefits of using modern technology in the manufacturing process.   3

    (d) Outline the factors that an organisation should consider before choosing a supplier.   3

                                                    Total marks   10

[END OF MODEL PAPER]

NATIONAL 5

2014

National Qualifications 2014

X710/75/01

Business Management

MONDAY, 19 MAY

1:00 PM – 2:30 PM

Total marks — 70

SECTION 1 — 30 marks

Attempt BOTH questions

SECTION 2 — 40 marks

Attempt ALL questions

Write your answers clearly in the answer booklet provided. In the answer booklet you must clearly identify the question number you are attempting.

Use **blue** or **black** ink.

You may use a calculator.

Before leaving the examination room you must give your answer booklet to the Invigilator; if you do not, you may lose all the marks for this paper.

MARKS

SECTION 1 — 30 marks

Attempt BOTH questions

It's All Wash and Go for Caroline

Caroline Gray opened Dogs Body Design in Kelso in 2013 with the help of the Prince's Scottish Youth Business Trust (PSYBT). Dogs Body Design provides dog grooming services and sells homemade treats, handmade dog coats and bandanas which are all made locally.

Caroline trained for a year before taking up a post in a dog grooming salon. She then managed a salon before deciding to set up her own business. The PSYBT provided a business advisor who helped her prepare a business plan and cash budget. They also gave a £5000 loan and a grant of £250.

The young entrepreneur's idea proved so successful in just her first couple of weeks that she employed a member of staff. Her popularity means she is fully booked up to a week in advance.

You should note that although the following questions are based on the case study above, you will need to make use of knowledge and understanding you have gained whilst studying the Course.

1. (a) (i) From the case study, identify **2** enterprising skills or qualities that Caroline has demonstrated. **2**

      (ii) Outline how these skills or qualities help Caroline develop her business. **2**

  (b) From the case study, compare the **2** types of finance provided by the PSYBT. **2**

  (c) Caroline provides a service to her customers.

     Justify the importance of providing good customer service. **2**

  (d) (i) Caroline employed a member of staff.

        Outline **3** stages in the recruitment process. **3**

      (ii) Describe the features of the Equality Act 2010. **2**

  (e) (i) From the case study, identify the stage of the product life cycle for Caroline's business. **1**

      (ii) Describe the stage identified in (e)(i). **1**

Total marks **15**

MARKS

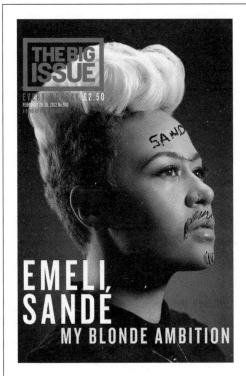

The Big Issue magazine was launched in 1991 by Gordon Roddick and John Bird in response to the problem of homelessness on the streets of London. The Big Issue aims to "help them to help themselves". The partners offer homeless people the opportunity to earn a legitimate income by becoming a vendor and selling magazines on the street. The vendor buys the magazine for £1.25 and sells it for £2.50.

Over twenty years later the organisation has helped thousands of vulnerable people to take control of their lives and currently works with around 2000 homeless people across the UK. The magazine has 63 distribution points nationwide.

The Big Issue is an example of a successful social enterprise. The magazine has clear social benefits and a reputation for getting exciting guest editors and exclusive celebrity contributions which has vastly increased sales.

You should note that although the following questions are based on the case study above, you will need to make use of knowledge and understanding you have gained whilst studying the Course.

2. (a) Compare the objectives of The Big Issue, identified from the case study, with those of a public sector organisation.   2

    (b) (i) From the case study, identify the method of promotion that is used by The Big Issue.   1

         (ii) Describe other methods of promotion that could be used by The Big Issue.   2

    (c) Explain how external factors could affect the success of The Big Issue.   3

    (d) The Big Issue could use rail to deliver its magazines to its distribution points nationwide.

         (i) Identify another method of distribution.   1

         (ii) State the advantages and disadvantages of this method.   3

    (e) Describe the factors to be considered when setting the price for The Big Issue.   3

Total marks   15

[Turn over

MARKS

SECTION 2 – 40 marks
Attempt ALL questions

3. (a) Discuss the advantages and disadvantages of recycling to an organisation.   4

    (b) Explain the problems of having too much stock.   2

    (c) The quality of products is important to all businesses.

        (i)   Identify **2** methods of ensuring quality.   2

        (ii) Describe the methods identified in (c)(i).   2

                                                    Total marks   10

4. (a) Define the following financial terms.
        • Fixed Costs
        • Variable Costs
        • Sales Revenue   3

    (b) Describe the actions that can be taken by an organisation to reduce costs.   3

    (c) (i)   Justify the use of a spreadsheet in the finance department.   2

        (ii) Describe the ways that other software can be used in the finance department.   2

                                                    Total marks   10

5. (a) Describe the selection process used to choose the right person for the job.   4

    (b) (i)   Outline **2** methods of industrial action.   2

        (ii) Explain the impact of industrial action on an organisation.   2

    (c) Compare piece-rate with time-rate as methods of calculating wages.   2

                                                    Total marks   10

MARKS

6. (a) Outline **2** internal factors that can affect the success of an organisation.

2

(b) Describe factors of production.

3

(c) (i) Identify **2** stakeholders of a supermarket.

2

(ii) Explain how these stakeholders could influence the success of the organisation.

3

Total marks 　10

[END OF QUESTION PAPER]

[BLANK PAGE]

DO NOT WRITE ON THIS PAGE

NATIONAL 5

2015

National Qualifications 2015

X710/75/11

Business Management

MONDAY, 11 MAY
1:00 PM – 2:30 PM

Total marks — 70

SECTION 1 — 30 marks

Attempt BOTH questions.

SECTION 2 — 40 marks

Attempt ALL questions.

Write your answers clearly in the answer booklet provided. In the answer booklet you must clearly identify the question number you are attempting.

Use **blue** or **black** ink.

You may use a calculator.

Before leaving the examination room you must give your answer booklet to the Invigilator; if you do not, you may lose all the marks for this paper.

MARKS

SECTION 1 — 30 marks

Attempt BOTH questions

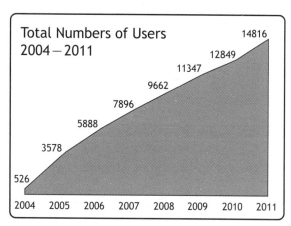

Total Numbers of Users
2004 — 2011

14816
12849
11347
9662
7896
5888
3578
526

2004 2005 2006 2007 2008 2009 2010 2011

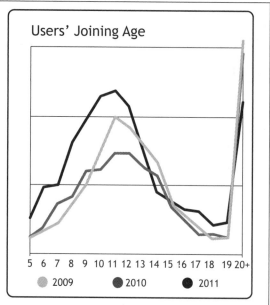

Users' Joining Age

5 6 7 8 9 10 11 12 13 14 15 16 17 18 19 20+

● 2009   ● 2010   ● 2011

The Factory Skatepark, based in Dundee, was recently named Social Enterprise of the Year. It offers extreme sports, youth and homework clubs, IT classes for the elderly and photography classes. It also has a sports shop and cafe.

The organisation is supported by grants from organisations including the People's Postcode Lottery, Comic Relief and the Big Lottery Fund. A major sponsor is Rockstar Energy drinks which is a favourite choice amongst teenage customers.

Factory Skatepark uses its website and social media to give information to customers and has launched an app to let members book sessions. Members are encouraged to give feedback to the organisation to help it meet its aims of improving customer service and finding interesting activities for all users.

You should note that although the following questions are based on the case study above, you will need to make use of knowledge and understanding you have gained whilst studying the Course.

1. (a) From the case study, identify **2** market segments that the organisation is targeting.   **2**

    (b) (i) From the case study, identify a charitable organisation that supports Factory Skatepark.   **1**

        (ii) Identify the sector of the economy that a charity would operate in.   **1**

        (iii) Describe **one** other sector of the economy.   **1**

    (c) Describe the features of a social enterprise.   **2**

    (d) (i) Outline the ways in which the skatepark can gain customer feedback.   **2**

        (ii) Explain the benefits of good customer service to the skatepark.   **2**

MARKS

1. (continued)

   (e)   (i) From the case study, identify the ways in which technology is used in promoting the skatepark.   **2**

        (ii) Describe the benefits of using technology to promote the skatepark.   **2**

[Turn over

MARKS

Glasgow-based clothing manufacturer Trespass was proud to be the official casual uniform supplier to the 2014 Commonwealth Games. The business is run by brothers Afzal and Akmal Khushi who established the Trespass brand in 1984. The business is run as a private limited company.

The owners were pleased to mark the 30th anniversary of the brand with such an honour. They have a wide range of products for men, women and children and specialise in sportswear for active pursuits. Customers can buy products online as well as in Trespass stores and outdoor clothing suppliers such as Go Outdoors.

Trespass mass-produces its clothing and uses hi-tech production. This ensures that quality is a key focus. The company has stores worldwide and employs hundreds of staff. Trespass prides itself in having a happy workforce and provides an excellent training programme for staff.

GLASGOW 2014
XX COMMONWEALTH GAMES

You should note that although the following questions are based on the case study above, you will need to make use of knowledge and understanding you have gained whilst studying the Course.

2. (a) From the case study, identify a sector of industry in which Trespass operates. **1**

    (b) Describe the features of a private limited company. **2**

    (c) Explain the benefits to a business of having a strong brand. **2**

    (d) (i) From the case study, describe the method of production used. **1**

    (ii) Discuss the costs and benefits of using this method of production. **3**

    (e) Describe the methods that can be used to train employees in the business. **3**

    (f) Describe the interests of stakeholders identified in the case study. **3**

[Turn over for SECTION 2 on *Page six*

DO NOT WRITE ON THIS PAGE

MARKS

SECTION 2 — 40 marks

Attempt ALL questions

3. Maddy Taylor is the owner and only employee of a cake-making business called Charm Cakes. She has produced the following break-even chart based on sales of her standard cakes.

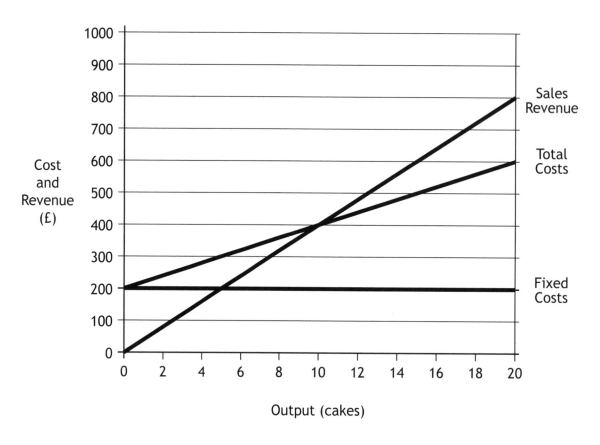

(a) From the break even chart, identify:

- the number of cakes sold at the Break-Even Point;
- Total Costs at Break-Even Point.   2

(b) From the chart, calculate the Variable Cost per Unit.   2

(c) Define the following terms.

- Break-Even
- Fixed Costs
- Variable Costs   3

(d) Justify the use of the following sources of finance:

- a bank loan;
- a grant;
- an overdraft.   3

MARKS

4. (a) Describe stages of the recruitment process.   4

    (b) Outline the role of technology when recruiting and selecting staff.   3

    (c) Describe the responsibilities of the employer under Health and Safety legislation.   3

5. (a) Describe the advantages of computerised stock control.   3

    (b) Describe how an operations department can be environmentally friendly.   2

    (c)   (i) Identify **2** quality inputs in the production process.   2

       (ii) Justify the importance of using good quality inputs in the production process.   3

6. (a) Promotion is an element of the marketing mix.

       (i) Describe the other elements of the marketing mix.   3

       (ii) Outline the methods of sales promotion which an organisation could use.   3

    (b) Discuss the costs and benefits of using desk research.   4

[END OF QUESTION PAPER]

[BLANK PAGE]

DO NOT WRITE ON THIS PAGE

NATIONAL 5

2016

National
Qualifications
2016

X710/75/11

Business Management

FRIDAY, 27 MAY
9:00 AM — 10:30 AM

Total marks — 70

SECTION 1 — 30 marks
Attempt BOTH questions.

SECTION 2 — 40 marks
Attempt ALL questions.

Write your answers clearly in the answer booklet provided. In the answer booklet you must clearly identify the question number you are attempting.

Use **blue** or **black** ink.

You may use a calculator.

Before leaving the examination room you must give your answer booklet to the Invigilator; if you do not, you may lose all the marks for this paper.

MARKS

SECTION 1 — 30 marks

Attempt BOTH questions

Question 1 of this paper replaces the original one in the SQA Past Paper 2016, which cannot be reproduced for copyright reasons. As such, it should be stressed that it is not an official SQA-verified section, although every care has been taken by the Publishers to ensure that it offers appropriate practice material for National 5 Business Management.

Just Dogs

Just Dogs was established in December 2006 by Gemma Johnstone. As a devoted dog owner and dog lover Gemma wanted to offer "doggy" people the chance to visit a shop that would offer a great selection of quality and unique dog accessories and supplies. Whilst the online doggy market proves popular, Gemma wanted to give dog owners the opportunity to be able to visit the shop, see the products and try them out before purchasing. Gemma also likes to be on hand to offer advice and tips to customers who visit the shop, which is based in Edinburgh.

Gemma is currently studying towards the Advanced Diploma in Canine Behaviour. This means that she is able to provide competent advice regarding dog training, behaviour and nutrition. It is important to Gemma to be able to offer a personal, tailored service to customers and this is central to the way the business is operated.

Just Dogs promotes responsible dog ownership. All of its practical doggy products are accompanied with useful guidance, tips and messages. This allows owners to look after their dogs in the best possible manner.

Adapted from www.justdogsshop.co.uk

You should note that although the following questions are based on the case study above, you will need to make use of knowledge and understanding you have gained whilst studying the Course.

1. (a) (i) From the case study, identify the type of business that Gemma operates.   1

   (ii) Using information from the case study and knowledge that you have gained, give 2 examples of good customer service.   2

   (b) Describe 2 costs and 2 benefits to Gemma of operating a website as well as her shop.   4

   (c) Outline methods of promotion that Gemma could use for her business.   3

   (d) Gemma is undertaking training to help her provide a better service to her customers.

   Describe the benefits of staff training.   3

   (e) Describe 2 costs that Gemma may have in her business.   2

MARKS

Who Made Your Pants? is an ethical business that was launched in 2008 by Becky John because she really didn't like wearing clothes that were made in sweatshop conditions. The company makes underwear using traditional fabrics, like lycra and lace, which are bought from big underwear companies. These fabrics are unwanted materials which are normally thrown out as waste at the end of a season.

In 2014, Becky won Social Entrepreneur of the Year for her business that creates manufacturing jobs for women who have been excluded due to their status as refugees. She employs 8 women with refugee backgrounds from countries such as Sudan, Somalia and Afghanistan.

The company provides training and every new recruit starts by working on one style of underwear and then moves onto the more complicated styles. The pants are handmade and each woman has a specialist job like cutting, sewing or trimming so there will always be more than one person involved in the making of each piece of underwear. All profits the company makes go back into the business.

You should note that although the following questions are based on the case study above, you will need to make use of knowledge and understanding you have gained whilst studying the Course.

2. (a)   (i)   From the case study, identify **one** way that Who Made Your Pants is ethical in its production.   1

(ii) Justify the importance of ethical production.   3

(b) Who Made Your Pants sells its products online.

Explain the benefits of online selling (e-commerce).   3

(c)   (i)   Identify **one** type of training used by Who Made Your Pants.   1

(ii) Describe an advantage of the type of training identified in (c)(i).   1

(d) Describe the methods of selection that could be used by Who Made Your Pants.   3

(e) Describe the methods that Who Made Your Pants could use to ensure the quality of its underwear.   3

[Turn over

MARKS

SECTION 2 — 40 marks
Attempt ALL questions

3. (a) Internal factors can influence performance.

    (i) Identify **2** internal factors.   **2**

    (ii) Explain the influence of the factors identified in (a)(i).   **2**

  (b) Outline the objectives of a non-profit-making organisation.   **2**

  (c) Discuss the advantages and disadvantages of operating as a sole trader.   **4**

4. (a) Outline the ways an organisation could use the following technology in the recruitment and selection process.

    (i) Word processing package   **1**

    (ii) Database package   **1**

    (iii) Company website   **1**

  (b)   (i) Identify **2** methods of industrial action.   **2**

    (ii) Explain the impact of industrial action.   **3**

  (c) Outline the impact of technology on working practices.   **2**

[Turn over

MARKS

5. **Cash Budget for Green Energy Solutions Ltd**

	£ May	£ June	£ July
OPENING BALANCE	20,000	(3,000)	(2,000)
RECEIPTS			
Sales Revenue	2,000	8,000	13,000
TOTAL	22,000	5,000	11,000
PAYMENTS			
Purchases	1,000	2,000	3,500
Wages	3,000	4,000	4,000
Advertising	1,000	1,000	1,000
Purchase of Motor Van	20,000	0	0
TOTAL	25,000	7,000	8,500
CLOSING BALANCE	**(3,000)**	**(2,000)**	**2,500**

(a) (i) From the cash budget, identify **2** cash flow problems.   2

    (ii) Describe how the problems identified in part (a)(i) could be solved.   4

(b) From the cash budget, identify an example of:

    (i) a fixed cost;   1

    (ii) a variable cost.   1

(c) Outline the purposes of producing an income statement.   2

6. (a) Describe the methods of production.   3

(b) Outline the factors an organisation might consider when choosing a supplier.   3

(c) Explain the possible problems of:

    • under-stocking;

    • over-stocking.   4

[END OF QUESTION PAPER]

[BLANK PAGE]

DO NOT WRITE ON THIS PAGE

NATIONAL 5

Answers

NATIONAL 5 BUSINESS MANAGEMENT MODEL PAPER

Section 1

1. (a) (i) Market segments must be identified:
   - Under 17 tuition
   - Learner drivers
   - Corporate packages

   2

   (ii) • Higher level of sales
   - More opportunity to achieve profits
   - Helps the business grow/survive
   - Differentiation of product lines

   3

   (b) • Employees will be away from the workplace therefore no distractions
   - Employees will be more motivated and will be more likely to stay with the organisation
   - Off the job training can be expensive so will reduce the profits of the business
   - While the employee is away less work will get done meaning lower productivity

   4

   (c) • Customers can access 24/7
   - They can book lessons online
   - Can use the website to collect customer information
   - Provides advertising for the business
   - Will provide contact details for customers

   4

   (d) (i) Tertiary Sector

   1

   (ii) The provision of services

   1

   Total marks 15

2. (a) • They will have a better reputation
   - They will attract more customers
   - They will attract more sales
   - They may be able to charge higher prices

   3

   (b) (i) Quality measures must be identified from the case study given. Identifiable measures are:
   - Quality control
   - Quality assurance
   - Quality raw materials
   - Skilled and motivated employees
   - Regular audits

   2

   (ii) • Fewer customer complaints
   - Fewer returns
   - Happier customers

   2

   (c) • Job analysis — to identify the vacancy and establish what the job would entail
   - Job description — with details of the tasks involved in the job, responsibilities, pay and conditions etc.
   - Person specification — detail the skills, experience and personality required for the job
   - Advertise the job — internally or externally

   3

   (d) (i) Private Limited Company

   1

   (ii) • Owned by shareholders
   - Controlled by a Managing Director and Board of Directors
   - They will have limited liability
   - It will be easier to attract more finance

   2

   (e) • Shareholder/investor funds
   - Bank loan
   - Retained profits

   2

   Total marks 15

Section 2

3. (a) • Easy to obtain/organise
   - Can be paid back in installments
   - Can organise to suit cash flow
   - Do not lose control of the business

   2

   (b) • Rent
   - Insurance
   - Salaries

   2

   (c)

Sales	£280,000
Production costs	£120,000
Other expenses	£85,000
Gross Profit	*£160,000*
Net Profit	*£75,000*

   2

   (d) • Can identify times when there will be a cash shortfall
   - Can identify when cash will be available to buy fixed assets
   - Provides a plan for the future
   - Can set targets

   4

   Total marks 10

4. (a) • Application forms
   - Testing
   - Interview

   2

   (b) • Time Rate — paid per hour worked
   - Piece Rate — paid for each product made
   - Time Rate — doesn't reward those who produce more
   - Piece Rate — doesn't reward those who work longer hours

   2

   (c) • Gender
   - Race
   - Disability

   3

   (d) • To ensure safe working environment
   - All machinery is well maintained
   - Provide adequate training for employees
   - Ensure safety for members of the public

   3

   Total marks 10

5. (a)
- Development
- Introduction/Launch
- Growth
- Maturity
- Decline

4

(b)
- Observation — watching consumers' behaviour
- Interview — 2 way discussion with the consumer
- Telephone survey — phoning consumer at home
- Postal survey — sending questionnaires to the consumer at home

4

(c)
- Cost of production
- Competitors' prices
- The target market

2

Total marks 10

6. (a)
- The same machinery can be used for all varieties of soup — less capital expenditure
- Not enough demand for flow production — saves on waste
- Can vary production to meet market demand

2

(b)
- In quality control products are checked at the end of the process whereas they are checked at each stage with quality management.
- There is less waste/scrap with quality assurance than there is with quality control
- Quality management is more expensive to implement than quality control

2

(c)
- CAN/Robotics/automation will produce fewer errors/less waste
- More consistent production
- Reduces staff costs

3

(d)
- Quality
- Quantity
- Reliability
- Price

3

Total marks 10

NATIONAL 5 BUSINESS MANAGEMENT 2014

Questions that ask candidates to Describe . . .
Candidates must make a number of relevant, factual points up to the total mark allocation for the question. These should be key points. The points do not need to be in any particular order. Candidates may provide a number of straightforward points or a smaller number of developed points, or a combination of these.

Up to the total mark allocation for this question:
- 1 mark should be given for each accurate relevant point of knowledge.
- a second mark could be given for any point that is developed from the point of knowledge.

Questions that ask candidates to Explain . . .
Candidates must make a number of points that relate cause and effect and/or make the relationships between things clear, for example by showing connections between a process/situation. These should be key reasons and may include theoretical concepts. There is no need to prioritise the reasons.

Candidates may provide a number of straightforward reasons or a smaller number of developed reasons, or a combination of these.

Up to the total mark allocation for this question:
- 1 mark should be given for each accurate relevant point of reason.
- a second mark could be given for any other point that is developed from the same reason.

Questions that ask candidates to Compare . . .
Candidates must demonstrate a true comparison in order to gain any mark. Both sides of the point must be clear but need not be linked. Candidates can write several points regarding the first comparison item followed by several points on the second and the marker match the points using codes (eg a, b, c).

Up to the total mark allocation for this question:
- 1 mark should be given for each compared point

Section 1

1. (a) (i) Identifiable skills and qualities from the case study. Responses could include:
- Caroline has completed training
- Caroline has experience in managing a salon
- Caroline has experience in dog grooming
- Communication
- Planning eg business plan
- Decision making skills
- Financial skills
- Risk taking
- Creativity/come up with an idea

(ii) Responses could include:
- Training – to provide her clients with a top quality service
- Managing a salon - able to manage the bookings and finance effectively
- Experienced in dog grooming - that she will be able to meet customer needs
  o Can train new staff to same high standard
- Communication skills – can build good relationships with customers or staff
  o Can make effective use of the business advisor

- Planning – can reduce the risk of failure
- Finance skills – so that she can avoid overspending

(b) Responses could include:
- A grant is money that does not need to be repaid whereas a loan is money that must be repaid
- With a grant no interest is incurred but with a loan interest will be added to the amount owed
- A grant is usually a one off payment whereas a loan can be requested several times
- Both types of finance from external sources

(c) Responses could include:
- Will ensure that customers return
  - o This will increase the sales of the company
- Caroline will gain a good reputation
  - o Which will entice new customers to try her business
- Caroline will be able to charge higher prices
- Customers will recommend to friends/family
- Caroline may receive fewer complaints from customers

(d) (i) Responses could include:
- Identify the vacancy
- Carry out a job analysis
- Create a job description
- Create a person specification
- Advertise the job
- Send out application forms

(ii) Responses could include:
- The Equality Act 2010 simplifies the current discrimination laws and puts them all together in one piece of legislation
- Any mention of the 9 protected characteristics
- Now includes workplace victimisation, harassment and bullying
- Prevents discrimination

(e) (i) Identifiable stage:
- Growth
- Maturity

(ii) Responses could include:
- Growth – customers' awareness of the product increases/sales start to grow sharply
- Maturity – sales have reached their peak/she is fully booked up

2. (a) Identifiable objectives from the case study. Responses could include:
- The Big Issue has the objective to reduce homelessness whereas a public sector organisation has the objective to provide a service to a community
- Help homeless people earn a legitimate income whereas a public sector organisation has the objective to provide benefits for those in need
- Both the Big Issue and public sector organisations have the objective to make a difference
- The Big Issue has an objective to make a profit whereas a public sector organisation has the objective to use public funds effectively
- The Big Issue has an objective to increase awareness/sales whereas public sector organisation has the objective to provide a service
- Both organisations have the objective to be socially responsible

(b) (i) Identifiable method of promotion:
- Celebrity Endorsement/Celebrity Contributions

(ii) Responses could include:
- BOGOF – buy one get one free
- Free features – buy the product and get a complimentary product with it
- Discount for a limited time eg 25% extra
- Competitions – buy the product and enter a competition to win a prize
- Product endorsement…
- Fundraiser…
- TV advertising – producing audio-visual images to give information during commercial breaks
- Radio advertising – producing a radio advert sometimes with catchy tunes that can be played on local or national radio stations
- Newspaper/magazine advertising – images and information can be printed in local or national papers
- Outdoor media/billboards/transport – large images can be shown in prominent place/on the move
- Big Issue website – using their own website can give lots of information on their magazine and up and coming stories

(c) Responses could include:
Political
- Changes in laws may prevent the magazine from publishing certain stories
- Local councils may refuse to give vendors licences to sell on the streets

Economic
- There may be a reduction in consumer spending due to the recession
- Cost of producing the magazine may increase due to inflation

Social
- There may be greater sympathy to homelessness which could increase sales of The Big Issue

Technological
- The growth in electronic newsstands/apps may lead to a decrease in demand for paper magazines

Environmental
- The weather eg heavy snow may prevent vendors from being able to go to their pitch to sell The Big Issue
- Road works may mean delivery of the magazine is late in arriving from the distribution points

Competition
- Competition from other magazines may mean that The Big Issue loses sales
- Other charity organisations do street/shop donations may take money away from Big Issue vendors

(d) (i) Responses could include:
- Air – plane
- Road – van, lorry, car
- Sea – boat
- Pipeline
- Electronic

(ii) Responses could include:
- **Air**
  - o Provides fast transportation worldwide
  - o Can be affected by weather/delays
  - o Is relatively expensive
  - o Not direct – another mode of transport is required when the delivery reaches the airport

- **Road**
  - o Allows door-to-door delivery
  - o Can depart at any time/24 hours
  - o Restrictions to the number of hours a lorry driver can work
  - o Petrol prices increases makes this more expensive

- **Sea**
  - o It is more environmentally friendly
  - o Can handle bulky goods
  - o Goods may require additional road haulage to arrive at final destination
  - o Slower method of transportation than others

- **Pipeline...**
- **Electronic...**

(e) Responses could include:
- Profit to be made
- Cost of production
  - o These may include materials and labour costs
- Price of other magazines/competitors
- Image to be generated
  - o More up-market image may mean a higher price is charged
- Income to be provided to vendors
- Target market
- What customers are willing to pay
- Break-even point
- Demand ...

Section 2

3. (a) Responses could include:
Advantages
- Item can be reused to make new products
- Takes less energy to recycle than to extract new materials
- Limits the items ending up in landfills
  - o Reduces cost of landfills as fewer are required
  - o Improves the image of an organisation
- May be cheaper to produce using recycled materials
- Can give a competitive edge

Disadvantages
- Need to be sorted into different categories which takes time to do
- Some items can only be recycled a limited amount of times ie paper
- May be seen as inferior
- May reduce quality

(b) Responses could include:
- Money tied up in stock which could be used to improve another area
- Goods may deteriorate which could lead to high wastage costs
- Greater chance of theft which could mean loss of profit from unsold goods
- Greater storage/insurance costs which could mean prices may need to rise

- Goods may become obsolete - this wastes money as no-one is willing to buy

(c) (i) Responses could include:
- Quality Circles
- Benchmarking
- Quality Assurance
- Total Quality Management
- Quality Control
- Quality Standards
- Quality Inputs **(each separate)**
  Quality raw materials; training of staff; maintenance of machinery/equipment

(ii) Responses could include:
Quality Circles
- Small group of employees who meet regularly to discuss how to improve methods of working

Benchmarking
- Trying to match the standard of the quality leader/competitor

Quality Assurance
- To ensure 'right first time' and prevent errors
- Checking at every stage of the production process

Total Quality Management
- Continuous process where each employee takes responsibility to ensure quality is consistent with every product

Quality Control
- Checks at the beginning and end of the production process only

Quality Standards
- When the product reaches the required standard it can be awarded a quality logo
- Give customers confidence

Quality Inputs – each separate
- Raw materials need to be of quality in order to obtain a quality final product
- All staff must be trained so they are competent and are all working to the same quality standards
- Machines need to be maintained so that they do not make mistakes affecting quality

4. (a) Responses could include:
- Fixed Costs – costs which do not vary with output or sales
- Variable Costs – costs which do vary with output or sales
- Sales Revenue – the income received from sale of goods/services

(b) Responses could include:
- Change to cheaper supplier/new supplier
  - o Look to see if you can get bulk buying discount
- Reduce wages
  - o Cut overtime
  - o Release temporary staff
- Reduce utilities usage
  - o Move to energy saving light bulbs
  - o Fit sensors to switch lights off after a period of time of no motion
- Reduce advertising/switch to cheaper methods
  - o Set up own website
  - o Send adverts through e-mail
  - o Advertise in newspapers rather than on TV
- Move to cheaper premises to reduce rent

- Improve budgeting
- Use machinery instead of employees (automation)
- Hire purchase/leasing to spread payments

(c) (i) Responses could include:
- Formulae can be used to calculate information
  o Allows for automatic calculation if anything changes
  o Reduces error
- Information can be saved and edited later
- Templates can be used for financial information – eg Cash Budgets/Profit Statements
  o Standardisation of documents means that processes are easily replicated
- Graphs/Charts can be created to display information
  o Allows easier comparison of difficult financial information

(ii) Responses could include:
- Word Processing – to create documents informing departments of their annual budget figure
- Word Processing – to compile the Shareholders' Annual Financial Report
- Database – to keep records of suppliers' accounts due and/or debtors' accounts owed
- Database – to create reports of overdue accounts
- PowerPoint – to display financial information at the shareholders meeting
- Internet/website/online...

5. (a) Responses could include:
- Collect CVs/application forms
- Creating a short list/leet of suitable applicants
  o Compare the application forms to the job and person specification
  o Seek references from previous employers
- Interviews on a one-to-one or panel basis
  o Asking each potential employee a series of questions to allow for comparison
- Testing to provide additional information as to a candidate's suitability
  o Attainment – demonstrates skills
  o Aptitude – natural abilities
  o Intelligence – mental ability
- Successful candidate(s) informed/make the final choice
- Unsuccessful candidate(s) informed

(b) (i) Responses could include:
- **Sit in** – employees remain in the workplace but do not work
- **Overtime ban** – employees refuse to work overtime
- **Work to rule** – employees only undertake tasks stated in their job description
- **Go slow** – employees produce work at a slower rate
- **Strike** – last resort, where employees withdraw labour/refuse to work
  o Often accompanied by demonstrations, marches and a picket line
- **Withdrawal of overtime** – employer removes the opportunity for employees to work overtime
- **Lock out** – employees are locked out of the business premises
- **Close** – last resort action where a factory or workplace is closed and relocated
- **Boycott...**

(ii) Responses could include:
- Production within the organisation may come to a halt therefore the organisation could struggle to produce goods to meet customer demand
  o Causing customers to go elsewhere
  o Could damage the reputation of the organisation
- Delays in the production of goods can lead to loss of sales revenue as customers cancel orders
- Employees refusing to work overtime or going slow would slow down production
  o Creating a poor image or reputation
- Company's share price may fall due to the poor reputation of the firm
- Organisation may find it difficult to recruit staff as they have a poor image with potential employees

(c) Responses could include:
- Piece-rate is where they are paid by the units produced (or sales made) whereas time-rate is where employees are paid by the hour
- Piece-rate means the more units produced, the higher the pay whereas time-rate means the more hours worked the higher the pay
- Piece-rate means quality may suffer in order to get quantity whereas time-rate pay may result in a higher standard of output
- Piece-rate is often used for unskilled/factory workers whereas time-rate pay is used for skilled workers (could be flipped)

6. (a) Responses could include:
- Availability of finance
- Availability of staff
- Availability of time
- Experience/Training of staff
- Equipment available
- Current technology
- Quality of products
- Leadership/Quality of management

(b) Responses could include:
- **Land** – this refers to all natural resources
  o This includes farmland, water and coal
  o The reward for land is rent
- **Labour** – this is the workforce (employees)
  o The reward for labour is wages
- **Capital** – these are man-made resources
  o This includes premises, equipment, machinery
  o The money invested in the organisation
  o The reward for capital is interest
- **Enterprise** – the idea for the business
  o The person who brings together the other 3 factors of production
  o The reward for enterprise is profit

(c) (i) Responses could include:
- Owners/Shareholders
- Employees
- Managers
- Suppliers
- Lenders/Creditors
- Government
- Local Community
- Customers
- Pressure Groups

(ii) Responses could include:

Owners
- Make major decisions which can lead to mistakes being made resulting in less profit
- Can vary their level of investment which will impact the decision the organisation can make

Employees
- Can vary the quality of the work they produce which may result in wastage or complaints
- Can carry out industrial action which will impact on the amount being produced

Suppliers
- Can vary the quality of their supplies which affects the quality of final product
- Can delay delivery which will halt production

Lenders/Creditors
- Can vary the level of interest applied to loans which could make them more affordable
- Set the time frame for repayment which will affect the cash outflows every month

Government
- Can change legislation which may cost the organisation more money to implement
- Can change council policies/restrictions which make it easier for the organisation to gain planning permission

Local community
- Can protest about the actions of an organisation which can influence their image

Customers
- Can take their custom elsewhere which influences the organisation's level of sales

Pressure Groups
- Can protest against the organisation's decisions/policies causing questions to be raised by the public

NATIONAL 5 BUSINESS MANAGEMENT 2015

Questions that ask candidates to Describe . . .
Candidates must make a number of relevant, factual points up to the total mark allocation for the question. These should be key points. The points do not need to be in any particular order. Candidates may provide a number of straightforward points or a smaller number of developed points, or a combination of these.

Up to the total mark allocation for this question:
- 1 mark should be given for each accurate relevant point of knowledge.
- a second mark could be given for any point that is developed from the point of knowledge.

Questions that ask candidates to Explain . . .
Candidates must make a number of points that relate cause and effect and/or make the relationships between things clear, for example by showing connections between a process/situation. These should be key reasons and may include theoretical concepts. There is no need to prioritise the reasons.
Candidates may provide a number of straightforward reasons or a smaller number of developed reasons, or a combination of these.

Up to the total mark allocation for this question:
- 1 mark should be given for each accurate relevant point of reason.
- a second mark could be given for any other point that is developed from the same reason.

Questions that ask candidates to Discuss . . .
Where question asks candidates to discuss advantages and disadvantages they must make a number of relevant advantages and disadvantages up to the total mark allocation for the question. However, where question is only discuss this invites positives and negatives but does not insist on both.

Up to the total mark allocation for this question:
- 1 mark should be given for each advantage/disadvantage.

Section 1

1. (a) Identifiable market segments:
   - Age (only accept one example, eg youth)
   - Hobby/Interest
   - Location (Dundee)
   - Education

   (b) (i) Identifiable charitable organisations:
       - People's Postcode Lottery
       - Comic Relief
       - Big Lottery Fund

       (ii) Response should be:
       - Third
       - Voluntary

       (iii) Responses could include:
       Private Sector
       - Organisations owned by private individuals
       - Aim to make a profit

       Public Sector
       - Organisations owned and controlled by the government or local authorities
       - Financed by taxes

   (c) Responses could include:
       - Can be a profit making organisation
       - Uses its profits to help its cause

- Primarily has social or environmental aims
- Provide community benefits
- Job creation
- Funded by grants and sponsorship
- Has employees and volunteers
- Operates in the third/voluntary sector

(d) (i) Responses could include:
- Ask customers opinions/interview customers
- Place suggestions box in centre
- Post a survey/questionnaire to their home
- Create a feedback section on website
- Set up a focus group
- Feedback form

(ii) Responses could include:
- Good customer recommendations which may lead to higher market share
- Returning customers which increases sales/profits
- Increased customer loyalty which makes it easier to promote new products
- Improved reputation which attracts more customers or allows for higher prices to be charged
- Improved customer satisfaction which means customers may return

(e) (i) Identifiable methods of promotion:
- Smartphone/Tablet app
- Website
- Social media — eg Facebook/Twitter

(ii) Responses could include:
- Allows for communication 24/7
- Communication is possible all over the world
- Communication is faster/instant
- A more cost effective way of promoting the organisation
- Can pass on large volumes of information through the website or e-mail
- Can target potential customers more easily
- Creates a good image for the target market

2. (a) Identifiable sector of industry:
- Secondary sector
- Tertiary sector

(b) Responses could include:
- A business which is owned by a shareholder(s)
- Shares are not traded on the stock market/sold privately
- Run by a board of directors
- Incorporated — separate legal identity from owners
- Limited liability for owners

(c) Responses could include:
- Brand loyalty which means you are guaranteed returning customers
- Brand recognition so less advertising required
- Gives an illusion/image of quality which means higher prices can be charged
- Easier to launch new products due to customers being familiar with the brand

(d) (i) Identifiable methods of production:
- Flow production — products are made in stages on a production/assembly line
- Batch production — products are made in groups where one group of products are made together before another group is started

(ii) Responses could include:
Flow
- Fast rate of production
  o Allows organisation to cope with demand
- Manufacturing costs are reduced
  o Allows for more profits to be made
- Mechanisation/automation can be used
  o Fewer staff wages need to be paid
- Standardisation of products
  o Fewer complaints as all products are identical
- Economies of scale can be gained
  o Discounts from bulk buying would be possible
- Machine break-down can halt production
  o Leads to unhappy customers/loss of custom
- Lack of variety of products
  o Customers may not pay a premium price for mass produced goods

Batch
- Variety of products can be produced
  o Can meet customers specifications to a degree
- Economies of scale can be gained
- Mechanisation/automation can be used
- All products in batch are identical
- Equipment must be cleaned between batches
  o Slows production down

(e) Responses could include:
- Cascading — employees cascade training information to colleagues
- Role Play — acting out or demonstrating a role or scenario to provide a demonstration of how to perform under particular conditions
- Coaching — being taken through a task step by step and helped by a trainer or a coach
- Demonstration — trainee watches a task being demonstrated and then completes it themselves
- Induction training — new employees are trained when they first start in an organisation
  o Usually training on health and safety, procedures of the organisation
- On-the-job training — employees are trained in the workplace whilst carrying out the job
  o This could be done by shadowing a colleague
  o Employee learns the processes specific to the organisation
- Off-the-job training — employees are trained away from the workplace
  o This could be at a training centre or college
  o Employees are trained by experts

(f) Identifiable stakeholders are as follows. Responses could include:
Owners/Shareholders
- Level of profits they earn
- Image of the organisation
- Dividends/return on investment

Staff
- Level of pay
- Good working conditions
- Job security

Customers/Commonwealth Committee
- High quality products for best possible price/value for money
- Regular/consistent supply of goods
- Customer service provided

Section 2

3. (a) No of cakes at BEP – 10 cakes
Total Costs at BEP – £400

(b) Variable Cost per Unit:
Total Costs – Fixed Costs = Variable Costs
£400 – £200 = £200
£200/10 units = £20 per unit

(c) Responses could include:

Break-Even
- Point at which Total Costs = Total Sales/Revenue
- Neither a Profit or a Loss is made as this is the point where sales cover costs

Fixed Costs
- Costs which do not vary with output or sales

Variable Costs
- Costs which vary directly with output or sales

(d) Responses could include:
Bank loan
- Paid back in instalments
- Paid over a long period of time

Grant
- Money does not need to be repaid

Overdraft
- Suitable for short-term cash flow problems
- Money available quickly as it can be prearranged
- Can take more money out than you have in your account

4. (a) Responses could include:
- Identify the vacancy (max 1)
- Carry out a job analysis, examine the vacancy to identify the tasks and skills of the position
- Create a job description, states the tasks and responsibilities of the job
  o Includes the conditions of the post eg pay, hours
- Create a person specification, the skills and qualifications the ideal candidate would possess
  o Essential and desirable characteristics can be defined within this document
- Advertise the job – to enable the vacancy to be seen by applicants either internally or externally.
  o Internally on the organisation's intranet, noticeboard etc
  o Externally in newspapers, job centres etc
- Send out application forms (max 1)

(b) Responses could include:
- Pre-employment online screening to assess the suitability of applicants
  o Identical basic questions for anyone who wishes to apply
  o Helps narrow down the list to those most suited
- Online application forms
- Internet job websites
- Online tests and assessments
  o This may be the first stage of selection before an interview
- Database to record details of interviewees
  o To search for potential candidates with a specific skill or qualification
- Telephone interviews through conference calling
- Video conferencing through smartphones
- Word processing to create application forms

(c) Responses could include:
- Make the workplace safe and prevent risks to health
  o Ensure that plant and machinery is maintained and safe to use
  o Make sure that all materials are handled, stored and used safely
  o Provide adequate first aid facilities
  o Make sure that all facilities meet health and safety requirements eg ventilation
  o Check that the correct work equipment is provided and is properly used and regularly maintained
  o Take precautions against the risks caused by flammable or explosive hazards, electrical equipment, noise and radiation
  o Avoid potentially dangerous work involving manual handling
  o Provide protective clothing or equipment free of charge
  o Ensure that the right warning signs are provided and looked after
  o Carry out risk assessments
- Create a Health and Safety policy
- Ensure Health and Safety training is conducted regularly
  o When new legislation is issued
  o Regular reminders eg evacuation procedures

5. (a) Responses could include:
- Will avoid over-stocking and under-stocking
  o As stock levels will be known at all times
- Reduces the need for stock-taking
- Can be linked to supplier to order goods
- Can identify best sellers/non-movers
  o Which will help managers make decisions on promotions
- Up-to-date stock levels can be found instantly
  o Providing customers with accurate information
- Stock can be re-ordered automatically when the re-order level is reached
- Allows the organisation to keep track of stock rotation dates/perishable items
- Large amounts of information can be generated
  o That is useful for decision making purposes
  o Can search through large amounts of information quickly

(b) Responses could include any of the following:
- By reducing waste
  o This will help to reduce the amount of rubbish going to landfill sites
  o Using quality management processes
- By recycling packaging/waste products
  o To meet their environmental aims
- Solar panels/wind turbines could be used to help generate some of the electricity used in the production of products
  o This will reduce their energy bills
- They could have special controls fitted to lights so they automatically switch off
  o This will help to reduce expenses for the organisation
- Organic raw materials can be used

(c) (i) Responses could include:
- (Quality) raw materials
- Trained staff
- Good recruitment and selection process
- Maintained equipment
- Up-to-date equipment

(ii) Responses could include:
- Quality raw materials will result in a high quality finished product
- Improve customer satisfaction
  o Customers are likely to recommend products
- Helps to improve the image of the organisation
- Will reduce the number of accidents in the workplace
  o Can meet safety targets
- Fewer returns of faulty products
  o Reduces cost to the organisation

6. (a) (i) Responses could include:
Product
- To ensure the product/service meets the customer needs
- Packaging has to protect the product and make it appealing to the customer

Price
- What the customer has to pay for the product/service
- To set price to ensure the business covers its costs to make a profit
- If price too high customers may shop at competitors instead

Place
- Where the customer will purchase the good or service from
- Includes website, high street shop
- Distribution methods

(ii) Responses could include:
- BOGOF — buy one get one free
- Bonus packs — getting % extra for the same price
- Free gift within the packs
- Discounted prices for a limited period
- Free samples to encourage customers to try a product
- Loyalty cards — receive points for purchases
- Competitions to win prizes
- Celebrity endorsement whereby a celebrity is paid to use the product
  o Encourages fans of the celebrity to buy this to be like their hero

(b) Responses could include:
Costs
- The information may be out of date
  o This will mean the decision made on this may not be accurate
- All the information is available to all your competitors
  o The organisation does not have the competitive edge
- Information may be written from a bias point of view
  o As you are unsure of the reasons for gathering the information
- Information may not be relevant to the organisation's needs

Benefits
- Information already exists therefore quicker to obtain
- Large amounts of information available
- Relatively inexpensive to gather and obtain
  o Researchers do not need interview training
  o Time is not wasted standing in streets etc trying to get first hand information

NATIONAL 5 BUSINESS MANAGEMENT 2016

Questions that ask candidates to **Describe** . . .
Candidates must make a number of relevant, factual points up to the total mark allocation for the question. These should be key points. The points do not need to be in any particular order. Candidates may provide a number of straightforward points or a smaller number of developed points, or a combination of these.

Up to the total mark allocation for this question:
- 1 mark should be given for each accurate relevant point of knowledge.
- a second mark could be given for any point that is developed from the point of knowledge.

Questions that ask candidates to **Explain** . . .
Candidates must make a number of points that relate cause and effect and/or make the relationships between things clear, for example by showing connections between a process/situation. These should be key reasons and may include theoretical concepts. There is no need to prioritise the reasons.

Candidates may provide a number of straightforward reasons or a smaller number of developed reasons, or a combination of these.

Up to the total mark allocation for this question:
- 1 mark should be given for each accurate relevant point of reason.
- a second mark could be given for any other point that is developed from the same reason.

Section 1

1. (a) (i) Sole trader

(ii) Responses could include:
- From the case study – Gemma likes to offer a personal and tailored service to her customers to meet their needs
- Providing extra assistance to a customer to ensure that their needs are completely satisfied

(b) Responses could include:
Costs
- Web hosting
- Website development and maintenance
- Postage charges for sending out goods to customers

Benefits
- Increased market share
- Ability to operate nationally/internationally
- "Free" advertising

(c) Responses could include:
- Advertising, e.g. radio, newspaper
- Customer demonstrations
- Free offers
- Competitions
- Discounts

(d) Responses could include:
- Staff get better at their job
- Increased motivation
- It is easier to introduce changes
- The image of the organisation is improved
- Staff become more flexible

(e) Responses could include:
- Rent
- Electricity
- Business rates
- Advertising

2. (a) (i) Responses could include:
- It reuses unwanted materials
- It reduces the amount of waste going to landfill
- Employ refugees
- Not using 'sweatshop' conditions

(ii) Responses could include:
- Limits the amount of waste going to landfill
- Improves the image of the organisation
- Increases sales/profits
- Can be used as a USP
  o Can give a competitive edge
  o Can win awards
- Can reduce costs if waste materials are used

(b) Responses could include:
- Access to more customers thus chances of increased market share/profit
- Access to customer information thereby allowing it to target products/marketing to those most likely to buy
- Can gain customer feedback thereby can change things to gain better customer satisfaction
- Customers can shop 24/7 which gives the organisation maximum time for customers to buy
- Can show entire product line thereby increasing customer choice
- Reduces costs as fixtures and fittings for shops are not required

(c) (i) Responses could include:
- On the job
- Induction training

(ii) Responses could include:
On the job
- Employees become familiar with surroundings
- May be cheaper than other forms of training
- Employees are actually productive
- Tailored to company needs

Induction
- Employees will feel at ease
- Employees will become familiar with the people and the surroundings
- Employees will become aware of health and safety issues

(d) Responses could include:
Application Form/CV
- These contain personal information on a candidate
- They can be used to compare against the person specification

Interview
- Allows the organisation to ask a series of questions
  o To allow for comparisons
- Allows the organisation to assess the candidate's appearance/personality
- Allows them to question the content of the CV/application form
- Allows a candidate to ask questions

Reference
- Provides key information on attendance, attitude, time-keeping
- Usually written by a past employer

- Allows an organisation to confirm the content of a CV/application form

Testing
- These provide additional information on a candidate's suitability through practical assessment
- An organisation can see how a candidate copes under pressure

(e) Responses could include:
Quality Circles
- Small groups of employees who meet regularly to discuss how to improve methods of working

Quality Assurance
- Checking at every stage of the production process
  o To ensure 'right first time' and prevent errors

Quality Control
- Checking at the beginning and the end of production process only

Quality Standards
- When the product reaches the required standard it can be awarded a quality logo
  o Gives consumers confidence

Quality Inputs
- Raw materials need to be quality in order to obtain a quality final product
- All staff must be trained so they are competent and are all working to the same quality standards
- Machines need to be maintained so that they do not make mistakes affecting quality

Benchmarking
- Trying to match the standard of the quality leader/competitor

Section 2

3. (a) (i) Responses could include:
- Staff/HR
- Management/HR
- Finance
- Technology

(ii) Responses could include:
Staff
- If staff are trained they will be more productive
- If staff are more motivated they may produce a higher quality service
- If staff feel they have a say in decision making they may be more loyal to the organisation

Finance
- If there is a surplus of cash then the organisation may be able to make improvements
- If there is a lack of finance cost cutting measures need to be considered

Management
- If their objectives differ from the organisation's then the overall strategic aims of the business may not be met
- The quality of their decisions eg the range of goods they decide to stock can mean that the organisation improves customer satisfaction

Technology
- Having up-to-date technology will allow the organisation to produce quality products
- Having up-to-date technology may give the firm a competitive edge

(b) Responses could include:
- Provide a service to others
- Raise awareness of issues
- Better service for the community
- Creating a better reputation
- Ensuring finances are kept within budget
- Be socially responsible

(c) Responses could include:

Advantages
- The owner is hands-on to provide a personal service
- Owners get to keep all their profits
- Easy to set-up
  - o Fewer legal restrictions
- Can make all the decisions
  - o This is faster as no arguments

Disadvantages
- Limited access to finance
- No-one to consult or share ideas with
- Difficult to take time off for holidays or if off sick
- Liability is unlimited
  - o The owners may lose their personal possessions in order to meet the debts of the organisation

4. (a) (i) Reponses could include:

   Word processing package
   - Create a job advert/application form
   - Key in a job or person specification
   - Letter to applicants about interview/successful appointments/unsuccessful notification

   (ii) **Database package**
   - Record of applicants
   - Record of posts available

   (iii) **Company website**
   - Online application form
   - Electronic job and person specifications could be accessed online
   - Contact us feature to apply for jobs
   - Internal jobs could be posted on the website

(b) (i) Responses could include:
   - Sit in
   - Overtime ban
   - Work to rule
   - Go slow
   - Strike
   - Boycott
   - Lock out
   - Protest/picket line

   (ii) Responses could include:
   - Production within the organisation may come to a halt therefore the organisation could struggle to produce goods to meet customer demand
     - o Causing customers to go elsewhere
   - Decreased levels of production could damage the reputation of the organisation
   - An organisation could lose customers as goods not produced within an acceptable timescale
   - Employees refusing to work overtime or going slow would mean deadlines not met
     - o Creating a poor image or reputation
   - Company's share price may fall due to the poor reputation of the firm

(c) Responses could include:
   - Software packages with remote access allow flexible working arrangements

- Video conferencing allows meetings employees between different locations
  - o Less travel time and cost are incurred
- Email allows an employee to communicate with their job share partner/communicate with the office from home
  - o Easier access to others with the use of email
- Allows work to be completed outside of 'traditional' working hours
- Less office space required as staff may be working from home using laptops
- Electronic documents can be shared and stored on the cloud/intranet to be used out with the office

5. (a) (i) Responses could include:
   - Increasing wages
   - Increasing purchases
   - £20,000 spent on capital expenditure
   - Negative closing balance in May and June

   (ii) Responses could include:
   - Do not allow overtime
   - Reduce the number of workers to reduce wages
   - Find a cheaper supplier to reduce cost of purchases
     - o Negotiate discounts for bulk buying or prompt payment
   - Purchasing the van on hire purchase
     - o To spread payments
   - Lease or rent the van rather than buying it outright
   - Arrange for an overdraft to cover negative closing balance.
   - Take out a bank loan to boost receipts

(b) (i) Responses could include:
   - Advertising

   (ii) Responses could include:
   - Purchases
   - Wages

(c) Responses could include:
   - To calculate gross profit
   - To calculate the cost of sales
   - To show net sales
   - To calculate the total cost of expenses
   - To calculate profit for the year/net profit
   - To show other incomes
   - For legal reasons
   - To aid decision making
   - For tax reasons

6. (a) Responses could include:

   Job
   - Where a one off/unique product is made
   - Each job is started and finished before moving on to the next

   Batch
   - When groups of similar products are produced
   - Machinery is stopped, cleaned etc before being used for a different batch

   Flow
   - A continuous process is used and goods move along a production line from beginning to end
   - Large volumes can be made in a short period of time
   - Each product is identical

(b) Responses could include:
- Price reflects the quality given
- Quality of the raw materials is consistent
- Delivery time meets the needs of the organisation
- The supplier can deliver the correct quantity
- The level of credit being offered by the supplier
- The length of credit period being offered by the supplier
- Location of supplier as it will impact on delivery charges/time

(c) Responses could include:

Under stocking
- Becomes harder to cope with unexpected changes in demand which means customers may go elsewhere to purchase the product
  o If customers go elsewhere they may lose them completely and not just the one time
- Production may have to stop completely meaning paying for workers who aren't producing any goods
- Continually ordering or restocking can mean increased administration costs
  o Increased transport costs
- Increased unit costs due to not bulk buying

Over stocking
- Carry large amounts of stock will increase the cost of storage which reduces profit
  o May result in having to pay larger insurance costs
  o Increased security costs
- Capital is tied up in stock which means that the money cannot be used elsewhere
- The stock may deteriorate resulting in larger wastage costs
- Changes in trends and fashion will mean that stock might become obsolete and not be able to be sold
- Higher risk of theft as it is less obvious when stock has gone missing

Acknowledgements

Permission has been sought from all relevant copyright holders and Hodder Gibson is grateful for the use of the following:

An extract from http://roadwisedrivertraining.co.uk © Aberdeen Foyer (Model Paper page 2);
The logos for Aberdeen Foyer and Roadwise Driver Training © Aberdeen Foyer (Model Paper page 2);
An extract and logo from http://www.angussoftfruits.co.uk © Angus Soft Fruits Ltd (Model Paper page 3);
An image and text for Dogs Body Design, taken from 'The Southern Reporter' 22 February 2013 © Johnston Press PLC (2014 page 2);
The cover of 'The Big Issue' magazine from February 20-26, 2012 (No 988) © The Big Issue Foundation (2014 page 3);
An article adapted from http://www.bigissue.com/about-us and http://www.socialenterprise.org.uk/about/about-social-enterprise/FAQs/test-case-study/case-studies/big-issue © The Big Issue Foundation & Social Enterprise (2014 page 3);
Logo © The Factory Skatepark (2015 page 2);
Logo © Trespass (2015 page 4);
Logo © Commonwealth Games Federation (2015 page 4);
An extract and logo from http://www.justdogsshop.co.uk © Just Dogs (2016 page 2);
Logo © Who Made Your Pants/Becky John (2016 page 3).

Hodder Gibson would like to thank SQA for use of any past exam questions that may have been used in model papers, whether amended or in original form.